ROOMS *AND* THEIR AIRS

ROOMS AND THEIR AIRS

JODY GLADDING

milkweed
editions

Published 2009 by Milkweed Editions
Printed in Canada
Cover and interior design by Cathy Spengler
Cover illustration, "Rooms and Their Air," from
    The Medieval Health Handbook, courtesy George Braziller
The text of this book is set in Figural.
09 10 11 12 13   5 4 3 2 1
First Edition

Please turn to the back of this book for a list of the sustaining
funders of Milkweed Editions.

LIBRARY OF CONGRESS CATALOGING-IN-PUBLICATION DATA
Gladding, Jody
  Rooms and their airs / Jody Gladding. — 1st ed.
    p. cm.
  ISBN 978-1-57131-432-1 (pbk. : acid-free paper)
  I. Title.
  PS3557.L2914R66 2009
  811'.54—dc22
                                              2008029321
This book is printed on acid-free paper.

Contents

I

II

III

ROOMS *and* THEIR AIRS

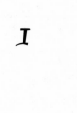

I've sold my parents' house

where
do their napkin rings
belong   what rooms
will I empty
where they are

not
they're not
everywhere tonight black
birds scatter gather
scatter again
nowhere

to roost   my grief
is that loose
flock   I
hoard the shiny
debris

Waders

1
Impossible   of course
              to step in the same river
                                                    twice
                    but sometimes   with hardly
                              a leg
                        to stand on
        I come back
                                        to test
                                              the shallows
                        and
the river
            offers
                        this foothold
                                        familiar bedrock
                      forever washed
            away
                                        in the rush
                    of
                              forever
                  coming
                                        to be.

2
Impossible   of course
              to step in the same river
                                                    twice
                    but
                                        just as impossible
        to step
                                              out—

Wolf Moon

that one cold fact
      — you are the one I chose —
   turning its stone face to us
                     all night

Vernal Pool

Why
        every year
                must I learn
        this lying low
                enough

                for the peepers
                        to flood with their
        calls sound
                        overflowing every depression in the night

                all   the   space   there   is
                but the space in me

            is snow melt
                        rain falling
        on deaf ears

                unless   I   listen
                                            hard.

Snow Moon Hunger Moon

the shoulder widens as the snow
begins to thaw along Route 14
a school bus drops off couples
draped across each other pine siskins
come for the salt outside the Quik
Stop they flock around the ice
cooler jackets undone kids grown
restless for the glint and bite
the crust dismantling this morning
the taste of snowmelt in our
water thin deer angled from their
beds before straggling into brush
the hollows they leave pregnant
my belly flared out like that
the first time I had sex was in
an old house through panes of
wavery glass broke a word for this
be/longing lit by nothing good
or evil the moon held sway
a bird feeder swung empty

Crow Moon

Flight
strikes crow
as such a good idea
she flaps and caws
at the thought
of it
meanwhile
overhead
hawk tilts a wing
mindlessly adjusting
the winds.

Up Hunger

Instead I climbed a mountain today, so the poem
I didn't write goes on too long and gets scrambly
near the top. Trees have fallen across it since the
last time—ice, I think. You can see my sister's house
through binoculars. It isn't finished yet, the floors
anyway, but the roof's already twelve years old and
needs to be replaced. Well we make/do because what
choice do we have. Here the poem climbs sharply up
      this   blue blaze   of sky   mountain   light—

April 17—Montagne Ste-Victoire

Perhaps the duty of consciousness in this regard is to be open to
a maximal realization, a delicate and precise awareness of one's
spatial relationship to the world.

—TIM ROBINSON, "ON THE CULTIVATION OF THE
COMPASS ROSE"

In Aix's Cathédrale St-Sauveur, what Aneleisa likes best are
the windows, high up, the only place light enters, though
filtered through colored glass, through story. Look, she says,
and look there, until we've turned full circle to admire each
wall's one eye, looking in.

Then, let's *go,* and outside, the unmediated sunshine makes
us blink. We've been talking about mountains, how we
are drawn to summits because it's there we can experience
ourselves as points in relation to the most possible space.
Because the idea of space, whatever inner space we know,
depends upon this corollary, its counterpart in the terrain,
to exist at all.

A corollary that escapes the whole construct of *sacred,* I
think, as we move away from this sanctuary of resonant,
arcing stone. Vaulted, because only space contained can
be hushed enough to fathom its own enormity.

Winds sweep the mountain, Ste-Victoire, its bare summit
exposed to bare sky. Aneleisa's exhausted herself on the
carousel and sleeps in the car as we stand along the road,

looking up and up. On the highest peak, the immense Croix de Provence looks spindly and misplaced. I follow the fold and wave of the sheer rock face as it drops to the Arc basin. Limestone, clay, tree line, wheat field. "The barest bones of the relationship between an individual and the world are topographical," the mapmaker Tom Robinson writes. "Our physical existence is at all times wrapped in the web of directions and distances that constitutes our space. Space, inescapable and all-sustaining. . . ."

When Aneleisa wakes, she's ready to climb.

My daughter asks why this is called *L'avenue de la Libération*
and trying to explain, my eyes fill with tears.

listen, Aneleisa—the cicadas
the way they fall silent as we advance
how we oppress them

no matter where in the world you walk,
this has already happened

Sap Moon

Finally
      she's the one to look to
when
      nothing it seems
                        will budge
                                    nothing
                  will ever go
                     right
                              again

                                          this wet nurse
call her
                        milk of kindness
call her
                        compassion, leaky old mother
                                    of love
         and she comes
                                    running
from underneath
                  to dissolve ice jams
                              thaw the pointing finger
            to set them loose again
                        all the many tongue-tied possibilities!

February 14—Dordogne

As for the first reindeer we have mentioned, it has no head: if we dismiss the hypothesis of deterioration . . . we may imagine the artist has not felt it had to be drawn or been attracted to doing so. Actually, the animal is about to pass round the rocky angle which bounds the scene . . .

—THE FONT-DE-GAUME CAVE

Which is not to say she's left anything unfinished, only that the processes of creation are ongoing. So she takes the pigment into her mouth. She mixes it with her spit. She finds the reindeer's flank, there, curving out from the wet stone. And through a bird's bone, she blows.

It's her breath that fixes the line to the sweating limestone wall. Fixes it, but only in the play of shadow and light. Because the illuminating flame is alive, too, fed on moss and animal fat. Her hollowed limestone lamp will bear the traces of combustion, the same black and red of the reindeer, when it's found twelve thousand years later.

As twelve thousand years later, the plant cover on the hillside above the cave determines the climate within, balancing the inward percolation in such a way that, unless carbon dioxide levels are altered by visitors, the paintings remain viable, unharmed.

The word *flanc* is masculine in French. But its meanings aren't. Flank, side, *l'enfant qu'elle portait dans son flanc*— the child she was carrying in her womb, *à flanc de colline*— on the hillside, slope. Out of this one word, the animal emerges from the earth, the woman sounds her note, the head passes beyond the rock boundary and into the light of day.

1

She slips free

So
her planted
body
pulls loose
shouldering down
root throat
into my other
mouth
head first
and bruised
glistening
she slips free
of all
I
meant
all I name.

2

She lies on my ribs

still so new
her breathing's unsure
as she rises
and falls with me
underneath her
ledge shifts
water surges
ground thaws
this first spring
with one ear
to the ground
she's learning to sleep
through anything.

3

She laughs

when Beth dies

because the earth
is mostly fluid

its abundant
indifference

cresting in waves
so faultlessly

through her I
hear myself break

into laughter.

4

She starts to walk

on equinox
because an egg
set on end
stays up
(not propped, no—
                    released!)

on her own
suddenly it's
my hands wavering
now where is
her need
to steady them?

5

She wants to sleep in her own bed

Through cloud cover
the moon rises late and small
enough light to see that it's raining in
no matter how hard nothing will draw
her close again tonight
I shut the windows.

6

She comes home sick

with a fever
her lunch uneaten
and falls asleep breathing fast
by the fire
though it's early September
there's no sun today
she warms
the house and her dreams
are the silence I work in
upstairs
all afternoon
a single shrill cricket.

7

She says the snow

is resting
on the trees
because it's tired

after falling
so fast

asleep

that long night
after her birth

she wakes
to plummet
through these branches.

8

She kneels out

the window bread crumbs
spilling from her
hand a finger raised
for that white pigeon
to land on *how come
you think she's not
tame*?

February 15—Dordogne

*Les gravures sont souvent incomplètes et parmi un véritable lacis
de traits et de signes, le visiteur peut, selon les angles d'éclairage,
lasser gambader son imagination.*
—SITES PRÉHISTORIQUES EN PÉRIGORD

Bernifal isn't open in winter, so our guide meets us in the
parking lot and we walk half a mile through woods to the
cave's entrance. He's forgotten his light, and while he goes
back for it, Aneleisa decides this cave's too much for her.
She and David wait outside while I enter.

Bernifal is a living cave, my guide explains, pointing out
the still forming stalactites and pools of water on the
cave floor. He wonders what I'd like to see—the horses?
the mammoths? the enigmatic symbols that may have
something to do with fertility? Since my only preference
is for the engravings rather than the paintings, he chooses
for me. His light traces an indentation I would have taken
for no more than an irregularity in the stone. *Dos, queue,
fesses, jambes, ventre, jambes, tête, naseaux, yeux, oreilles.* As he
names the body parts, a horse appears. We move on and
he points out the bear, the mountain goat, the human hand.

I can't help reaching up to touch the wet wall, and now,
it's six years earlier, the spring Aneleisa arrived, and I'm
running, maybe for the first time since giving birth. I'm
sweating and bleeding and I have to stop along the trail and
lean forward to keep my breasts from leaking through to
my T-shirt.

23

Stalactite. From the Greek *stalaktos,* dripping. *Gambader,* to gambol, leap, or frisk about. *Un lacis,* a network or web, milky way. Half seeing, half imagining here in the dark, we trace points of light to find creatures overhead. *Dos, jambes, ventre, tête.* A Stone-Age horse, a mother leaking milk, a living cave, a sky full of stars.

As we go out, the guide pauses at a small human face etched above us. *Un visage humain,* he says, *rare, très, très rare.*

Fossile

It's just that
        sometimes after the earth has no more tears

you stumble
        across this rough-edged
    surface, broken

      clean of fluency, thinking of salt,
        and maybe, if you listen, you pick up something

              embedded
       or *memorize,* or

      sometimes, just
        glint—

Lavande

I give and I give and what I can't give
gets wrung from me pressed flat between
husband and child she's crawled in coughing
it's too hot to sleep but they are
his ankles bone hard each cough
going right through me I turn
I turn as if I could unwind
I'm no clock in the morning my arms
are twisted around my neck my neck
twisted *mama you smell good* she nestles in
he draws a finger down my spine.

Champignon

So now that the light's gone, why
not consider the manifestations?
You think I'm not natural, the way
my dark question surfaces and disappears,
crops up you might say, only
where's the lit progress of grain?
Listen, if all else fails,
you can live on fear. There are times,
swallowing your disgust, you'll crave
my pleated belly,
my yeasty voice rising from
the depths to say don't die this time,
only dream, only tremble. And here,
in the leaf mold, you do.

Sprouting Grass Moon

Sometimes just opening
     a window
   to hear the air moving
    is enough

                not even wind

   sometimes after making love
   to lie very still
and listen for the slightest

    shift

   the wildness

        retreating

    the tongue coming
     so civilly
    to rest.

Flower Moon

So many of them look down look away
                              the early ones
          this isn't easy for them
                                   the trout lily the wild oats
               I was sowing then I didn't even know
                    the boy hired to watch the building site
               I showed him where the road ended
                    and the overgrown trail
               I brought him to the open abandoned place
               and lay down

trust trust say the limp wings of emerging moths
     the new leaves droop from trees and blush swearing they
          don't know anything yet anything almost sickly
               green
                              I lay down

                    and no harm
          came to me there
               no harm
          done though so often my good mother
waited up if my blouse was inside out she turned
shaking her white head
                              oh my love remember
                    this time of molting crabs
               when nothing can protect you
                    and nothing does.

Chives

between
the slow dying
    green
the difficult birth
there is this green
GREEN!
the summer!
      house thrust open
the pollinators' return

between
winter just past
     hollow
winter looming
     pointed
we rise from our cramped beds
in suspended disbelief
        to people
the generous myth of summer!
its acrid largess

Watching wings emerge from a chrysalid, I see why
l'idée must be feminine.

Because how else
to engender
the other
except by comprising
what one
couldn't have
conceived:

a woman gives birth
to a son:

thistle: down

Softwoods

We utter nothing
true high
among the needled
fictions we create
so many opportunities
for truth
as it happens
continually
not only up here

but also under growth
where we sink
down in bogs
filled
with resolve
nothing we utter
is true
still
we groan
gape
and push a new
thing out.

Light Years

What else to
become
after all
but a shadow
of your former
self
bent
on anything
attached to form
only by the light
shifting now
at angle's whim
easing
the stiffness left.

For Piano and Strings

In G minor
grief
is that high
note
sustained
then descending
the bows drawn
slower
than healing
meanwhile
at the broken
surface where business
must go on
so many little steps
for the restless
hands.

Sundial

My father
dead a year
is *late*
it seems
I wait
for him
to fall
like dead trees
I wait
to count
the rings
the days
I count
by hours
but see
how these dead
suns
light up
the sky
at night
I lose
my way
for measuring time.

Moth Hole

Years later I dream Beth is a ghost
                                        a pile of clothes
an illusion

                        an *illusion* I insist
            to Ed who was her husband

                but he gets it all wrong
        he thinks I mean she doesn't exist
        that's not what I mean at all

        picking up
                her sweater
            putting my arm
                                    through her sleeve—

Beam

How is it I'm becoming particle
solid tool with a few odd uses
even as I'm honed to nothing
more than gesture—wave
or stride, shrug, stutter?
Resolute contradiction, I'm worn
so smooth by now I should be able
to explain everything. So what
is it that escapes me, that
on good days, lifted and filled me?
Because *that's* what I
would have called light.

Hay Moon, Thunder Moon

Where
                    among the sunlit bales
            is there room for human grief

not here   not here   not here   not here   not here   not here

                    crickets sing till sky
cracks and down
            pour the ten thousand forms for it

                all lost
            on the indiscernible moon
                    even with her dark side
                            her different names—

Red Moon

       mid-August   windows rolled down   cigarette lit

    and it smells *good*   smells like freedom
I cooked at the steakhouse all summer
and slept late and lay hot and oiled in the sun
each afternoon he drove me to work
my mother squinted up at us she saw
how his eyes burned how he
loomed over her the slick
arc of his grin   he

    lit up in the parking lot hot tar still
bubbling engine running while I closed
down the grill bagged the charred
bits I unpinned my name tag he
knew of a peach orchard not
far the white peaches would be
ripe by now   I didn't smoke but I
love the emberred
      end of this:

 the red ash
    falling away

                 heat rising from us
so much shimmering   that moon
           no one could say it wasn't living
              no one could call it dust.

Homing

Thrushes gone, flocks
    assembling
          like so many impulses
      until a motion is defined
          a motion is carried, we say
hoping to see monarchs
      though I've been out in the milkweed
        a long time
      rubbing my legs against these stalks
  what dull instruments
      we are
          compared to bee, or
    black-winged locusts collecting
          their thoughts
    the way they whirr up
    it's clear
        trust rides low in the body
    as later, surely
  the moon does follow
no matter where
      I go
  I can never fall

out
of the universe
from almost anywhere
the northern sky
would look like this
but still
in my walking boots
trying to fathom the countless destinations
if I stay here, these stars
know
where to find
me.

Hunter's Moon

warms a bit of the rug the colors
make me glad I'm alive as the hours
pass it settles in different rooms
when I lean deep into the night
I can call it home

good dog
lay down here
beside
me with a
happy
sigh—

Asparagus (*Sparagus*)

"the fresh kind whose tips are turned downward toward the earth . . ."

Northerly Region (*Regio Septentrionalis*)

There's some danger here of being too
luminous, though not like in the east
where light must be subdued with heavy
foods. Still, snowbank, silver birch,
aluminum flashing. Also glint of silt
in shale. Also hubcap. Glare ice—
this makes everything so simple and so hard.
Today's town meeting. It's wild apples
and roadkill that inspire strength and
prudence. Where snow machines have
packed the springs, deer paw and find
good water. Your votes will keep
the cemetery mowed. There's danger,
too, for chests of small dimension.
Regulate excursions with great care.

Squash *(Cucurbite)*

Curb your excesses, for I change
and get absorbed too quickly.
See? Already I'm taken in.
Be like water, I told myself, strange
aspiration for a vegetable, but by nature
I was cold and humid. Now
I quench thirst. This makes me
useful, though primarily for the young
in southern regions. Here
in the north, I descend in torrents.
Please, as long as I'm pouring
my heart out, withhold your good opinions.
Your stooped, lanky form is beautiful
to me, but we've agreed to nothing
yet. Consider that I stem—
and stem *from*—longing. Your neutrality
can be preserved with saltwater
which frees the body if you add good clay
and bathe in it. Or if you sail.

Tasteless Melons *(Melones Insipidi)*

But you can see, can't you, how I've
inverted the world, turning it in
to myself? First the green rim,
then flesh, then a network of glistening
seeds, each one a nascent universe.
My nature? Cold and humid, but contained
by rind as dry as cantaloupe's.
Some days, so many strands draw in
on my attention, I forget to say,
it's nice, the way you touch my shoulder.
Tasteless melons have their danger: if I
cause you pain, it's because I forget
my surface. How pale and rough I must
seem to you, all ribs, a lifeless star.

Sweet Apples *(Poma Mala Dulcia)*

Their nature? Sanguine, warm and humid
as blood, and they comfort the heart.
Please help yourself. The name I can't
pronounce—something like *paradixani.*
Here, have a taste. I used to be less liberal.
I'd cling to them, think flesh of my flesh.
But where does that lead? Collapsed brown
mouths the deer won't eat, come winter.
Better to harvest while a tree still knows
how blossoming's a way to enter deep into
the world. Even though it leaves you
scatterbrained, a stubble of missed
connections. Or fruitful and worried
by every inching thing. Just look at them—
my sweet, sweet apples. Please eat
your fill. Oh, I expect the nerves will suffer.
But where's the danger that
can't be neutralized? For this, a little
rose-colored sugar is good, a little honey.

Anger *(Ira)*

Our accord's a ruin. One swipe
across the cutting board scatters it.
Away's where I'm going, and if that's
blood boiling, leave it on. The heart's
a saucepan, not a cauldron,
the pint-size heart. It can't harm
you unless you've made illicit decisions.
Have you made illicit decisions?
Grit your wisdom teeth and don't expect
to neutralize the dangers with philosophy.
This is not optimum. It doesn't enlarge.
The color is not restored.
Tasteless melons, chatting, vomit—each
has its usefulness, even chickpea soup.
So to stew in our own juices may loosen
our tongues or keep us lively,
but it's more suitable for the very old.
Unlike chicken eggs, it won't noticeably
increase coitus. Unlike coitus,
it won't preserve the species.

Dawdling *(Cessatio)*

Nature: To extend one's allotment of time, especially while walking or during a meal. *Optimum:* The flowing, nonbitter kind, as practiced by children, where there is strict correlation between the movements of the mind and of the body. *Usefulness:* For those desiring infinity, but not transcendence. *Dangers:* Causes itching in those with much to do. *Neutralization of the Dangers:* With cheese between courses; by listening, looking on, or participating with joy and accord.

Rooms and Their Airs *(Camere et Aer Ipsius)*

Air out the quilt. Down remembers
the wind.

Remake the bed. Down remembers
its nest.

Open a window for northerly winds
that have swept across sweet water.

Open a window. Rain falling
on good land is good for melancholy.

Prepare a fish. If the skin's not thick,
it lived in shallows that run among stones.

Eat fish with wine and raisins. Your thirst,
too, might be derived from grapes.

Conserve the bones. Nothing you do here
will be forgotten.

Travel Moon

      So what
is turning
               away
                    I'm off
           again
to witness the
           fall
      that each leaf does
                this
                I know
yet I could stand here
         among the beautiful
            wasted days
                      forever
                and not
          see a single one
                let go.

Beaver Moon

Beaver spreads her broad tail over the moon
   all month she does this
      she says   work work

her tail's gray
      damp
         from end to end
   she slaps it hard she says
         work work

the trees raise their bare arms
         their empty hands
   nothing for them to do now

     beaver gnaws away
  from every side
         what's left of the day's
     pure heartwood

     beaver leaves it standing
         little wonder
       little spool of light—

When Cold Moon

rose it was not
that bright rim
I knew
it was not that boat

cold moon scooped me hollow

a shaking cusp
cold moon sheared me to quick
left me
stuttering

have you no white heat of your own
cold moon cold moon
I
reflected
I
could see
my
breath

One Day

lily
orange on a green stem
studded with so many tenses
in which it has never opened
will never
open

opens
its mouth wide
from its yellow throat thrusts
all seven tongues into simple present
breaks into one
unfaltering

now

Purple Loosestrife

She's headed uphill
                            against traffic
        lugging the plant she's dug
                it's hot and her hair's come loose
the weight of it
                            unbalances
      her   the magenta spikes   bob
                    so lanky
            tufted with blossoms

                        you've got to admire
them
                        bright hitchhikers
            how they make their way

                        escaping cultivation
                                    so what if it's invasive
            she thinks
                        it's beautiful
                and she knows just the place for it
                                to go
                                            wild.

Notes

The epigraph for "February 15—Dordogne" translates:
"The engravings are often incomplete and among a veritable
network of traces and signs, the visitor can, according to
the angle of light, let the imagination frolic." —*Prehistoric
Sites in Périgord*

"Fossile" is for Gustaf Sobin.

"Softwoods" and "Light Years" are for Archie Ammons.

The poems in "Asparagus *(Sparagus)*" draw on *The Medieval
Health Handbook* (Braziller, 1976), a compilation of plates
from fourteenth-century manuscripts depicting the effects
of various foods, plants, waters, fibers, weather conditions,
climates, activities, and emotions on human health.

The moon poems take their titles from Native American
names for the months, and roughly follow a calendar year.

Acknowledgments

Grateful acknowledgment is made to the following
journals where these poems have appeared:

AGNI: "Beam"

CAFÉ REVIEW: "My daughter asks why . . . ," "Sap Moon"

CHICAGO REVIEW: "Northerly Region," "Dawdling,"
"Tasteless Melons"

ECOPOETICS: "Purple Loosestrife"

88: "Sprouting Grass Moon"

EPOCH: "She slips free" (as "So")

GRAND STREET: "She says the snow," "She wants to
sleep in her own bed," "She starts to walk"

HUNGER MOUNTAIN: "Flower Moon"

NORTHERN WOODLANDS: "One Day"

ORION: "Snow Moon Hunger Moon"

POETRY: "For Piano and Strings," "Softwoods"

PLOUGHSHARES : "Anger," "Squash," "Sweet Apples"

TERRA NOVA: "She lies on my ribs"

WILD EARTH: "Rooms and Their Airs"

Some poems appear in *Artichoke,* a chapbook published
by Chapiteau Press, 2000, and *The Moon Rose,* a letterpress
limited edition by Chester Creek Press, 2005.

Thanks to the Mrs. Giles Whiting Foundation for its
generous financial support.

About the Author

Poet and translator Jody Gladding won the Yale Series of Younger Poets Award for her first book, *Stone Crop*, published in 1993. Her poems have appeared widely, including in *ecopoetics, Orion, Ploughshares, Poetry, Wilderness Magazine,* and elsewhere. Her recent translations include *The Serpent of Stars* by Jean Giono and *Small Lives* by Pierre Michon (Archipelago, 2004 and 2008). She has been a Stegner Fellow at Stanford and Poet-in-Residence at The Frost Place, and has received a Whiting Writers Award and a Centre National du Livre de France Translation Grant. She lives in Vermont.

Milkweed Editions

Founded in 1979, Milkweed Editions is one of the largest
independent, nonprofit literary publishers in the United
States. Milkweed publishes with the intention of making
a humane impact on society, in the belief that good writing
can transform the human heart and spirit. Within this
mission, Milkweed publishes in four areas: fiction, nonfiction,
poetry, and children's literature for middle-grade readers.

Join Us

Milkweed depends on the generosity of foundations and
individuals like you, in addition to the sales of its books.
In an increasingly consolidated and bottom-line-driven
publishing world, your support allows us to select and
publish books on the basis of their literary quality and
the depth of their message. Please visit our Web site
(www.milkweed.org) or contact us at (800) 520-6455
to learn more about our donor program.

Milkweed Editions, a nonprofit publisher, gratefully acknowledges sustaining support from Anonymous; Emilie and Henry Buchwald; the Patrick and Aimee Butler Family Foundation; the Dougherty Family Foundation; the Ecolab Foundation; the General Mills Foundation; the Claire Giannini Fund; John and Joanne Gordon; William and Jeanne Grandy; the Jerome Foundation; Constance and Daniel Kunin; the Lerner Foundation; Sanders and Tasha Marvin; the McKnight Foundation; Mid-Continent Engineering; the Minnesota State Arts Board, through an appropriation by the Minnesota State Legislature, a grant from the Wells Fargo Foundation Minnesota, and a grant from the National Endowment for the Arts; Kelly Morrison and John Willoughby; the National Endowment for the Arts; the Navarre Corporation; Ann and Doug Ness; Ellen Sturgis; the Target Foundation; the James R. Thorpe Foundation; the Travelers Foundation; Moira and John Turner; Joanne and Phil Von Blon; Kathleen and Bill Wanner; and the W. M. Foundation.

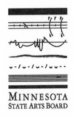

MINNESOTA
STATE ARTS BOARD

NATIONAL
ENDOWMENT
FOR THE ARTS
A great nation
deserves great art.

TARGET.

THE McKNIGHT FOUNDATION